Dear Jul

Thank you for the duck
It is such a pleasure
feelings to be friends

Love,

Zoh.

# UNION!

# СОЮЗ!

CANARIUM BOOKS
ANN ARBOR, IOWA CITY, SHANGHAI

SPONSORED BY
THE UNIVERSITY OF MICHIGAN
CREATIVE WRITING PROGRAM

# UNION!

ISH KLEIN

Canarium Books
Ann Arbor, Iowa City, Shanghai
www.canariumbooks.org

The editors gratefully acknowledge the
University of Michigan Creative Writing Program
for editorial assistance and generous support.

Cover and design by Gou Dao Niao

First edition

Printed in the United States of America

ISBN: 978-0-9822376-0-1

*For my friends, for anyone who needs what this is. This is yours.*

*Also, this book is in loving memory of Mrs. Frances Goldwater.*

# CONTENTS

## AMID OCEAN



## DRY LAND

## HARD EARTH



## UP AND AWAY!

# AMID OCEAN

## LITHUANIAN SUNSET

Ninety minutes since dark, I do not expect the surrounding ice
to quit its hold nor do I expect you wearied at my door:
shoulders narrow 'neath your dark green cloak.

You wouldn't be dashed by stones at my door
who take unkindly strangers; flinging them knee to split knee.
Dashed all strangers take me less than notable, even addled
as if they could win a contest to prove their contention.

I have wandered, am neither here nor there;
you are where I left: sous terre,
roiling voices beneath your brow
and beaux who wrote with forced arm; not strong.

This is to say meet me where I met you first.
Where you stirred as I lowered myself over cliff's edge.
A burgundy train I wore; you held me up by this.
Your great strength, a thing beside, a saviorial beast, loving.

I am the kind who need only be reminded of kindness
and with my All will pursue that quality in the new life.
The remembering one. You seemed to see this.
You lost your horse carelessly that day.

## WORLD'S END WITH SYMPATHY

Some time ago was I, mid-ocean, lost
with dog. Unfortunate, drifting board
to board until a skiff of three survivors
did like our shades enough to save them.
So we boarded by her hand's extent.
That laughing lady filled with liquor.
Not befouled by spirit. She took fine liking
by our sides, made us warm,
welcomed by the other two.
At first I said nothing.
Held close my mutt, Maelstrom, and drank
and drank free from sea's ill-considerate current.
It was three months' hard rain,
then everything under.

The shakes of days
was within me.
Waving gnawing fish from flaked flesh,
and night terrors
(I could not speak) of bigger bullies
who tried their turns.
For sharks I'd feign bloodless
well enough to wonder, deep down,
had I drowned?
Or times I could not find my dog immediately,
or if gulls got near him
I would scream them away,
scaring all of us that way.

She who found us, called Beatrice, calmed us.
Her hand light over my head,
the dog on the floor,
there were two others next to me.

By heart and eyes pretending sleep were we.
But she was voicing joys:
Italians she'd well known,
light through her old red windows in the afternoon,
tea with her own grandmother,
the Easter season …
These things startled us.
We didn't know how to say.
Mouth opens, nod, next some sounds.

The wild kids beside me
drew their latest history on the floor before us.
(One girl, one boy.) They came from a castle
where they had room and board
but their lord did not believe them.
They'd sulk to the scullery,
put fists through festival cakes,
pour out all the milk—nothing.
Lord Roland said it was rats.
They hated him for taking them
out of their forest, shaving their heads,
getting them used to sugar and shoes
then forgetting them.

Water rose before revenge.
They intended to saw off his ears
(his prized possessions) then feed them to the hogs.
But he'd been dead all along.
Some captor: face of lacquer, his brains
just sawdust showing through a gap
in his hatless head.
They wanted to be forgiven for his effect on them.
They waited at the battlement for the water's takeaway
but they would not be put under
and soon stopped trying to sink.
The boat found them holding fast to a tree limb

from the forest that started them.

Days we'd stretch and scrape salt from our skin,
night opened so gently
like a curtain to a picture showing
lights from satellites the likes of me
had never known before.
Something taking us away—
Bodies cagier by the day.
Evening musings would be so occupying
then they'd leave, spirited—
to populate dry land somewhere?
To guide with stars our craft?
My dog shaking the fish in his mouth
after I'd ripped the bones out.
The girl holding her hand over his thrumping tail.

There was nobody else in the water (we'd all always look).
I was curious to know where my friend ended up.
She comes back in dreams.
I see her planning her Entrance, her break into fame.
We went in together, a while back.
I was supposed to do something, I couldn't hear.
Then, quickly, she caught the circular current.
It goes around once then you go down.
It was shocking, her taking that same way as those others
who did not seem nearly as buoyant.
But the thing that takes you down; it wants what it wants.
It knew the worth of this person.
She is a jewel in the wall of the underworld
that keeps souls from despairing.

I suppose
too, she is a jewel
in my brain's own
undercurrent,

amid all the ugly and
unfortunately
remembered she has been
the Bright Relief
of what can be.
The light through
her is how it all
gets beautiful.
I've seen this so I know.

## YOU ARE HERE

According to the parchment,
thin lines connect us through seas
deep enough for giant squid.

We know there are squid because their dead bodies wash up.
Otherwise, they eschew us; the squids do. Married to mystery,
God told them: avoid all gawkers.

Who are us; we are here looking and as separate continents
try to love one another though jagged coastlines discourage trade
and belabor analogies.

When I thought I was original I was wrong,
I was only alone. Near me, God said,
"You are here finally little miracle! My one and only!"

"Yes I am here!" I said.
"No, not you! I meant,
She whose glee cannot be contained within a face!"
He meant the girl with the cleft palate beside me,

she was hiding. A deep being hiding.
Excusing herself as humans do; creatures of shame;
it is difficult to escape this fate.

We tell ourselves one thing,
people oppose it. The crusty world agrees with them.
We are here. I am sorry. Always

in America: home of the freeze and land of the blame!
I am here similar to nothing. Someday I will be something,
something will become of the perpetual space,

the American mind which is like a clever simile:
trust me. It's as blank as a blank.
I am broken free

all the way out and about.
In the Capitol
a star

between places where we meet while we are moving:
through blood, through lines,
we see stars, and breathe sky.

# MY LOVE HAS LEFT ME I HAVE NO HOME

It's been iffy.
And yes, it's my own damn fault.
The Ignorance!

They (my keepers) didn't know, so how could I know?

In any case, I've been active in my shell—
like existence.
Now I know!

Love can be lost.
The host is often out to lunch
or an unwitting zombie

since supermen can get us
to do most anything
in our innocence

or let me just say my innocence—
they got ME in MY INNOCENCE.
And when I say innocence, I mean ignorance.

Now, out of synch with all but three things.
That I dream and that I am a dream and that without my love
my soul runs into the sun. Hey, wait for me! But no. It is a crazy mofo.

I am left here. I hid myself from God (the Silent),
I thought he was a superman: a boss.
I desired and hated the slavery vis-à-vis all these forms about my head.

And I know he or it knows where my love went
but he or it won't say this
in direct human English.

So I can't tell the curb from the street.
Fast metal with wheels and lights Lethal!
This phase has most days seen me behind a boundary

I'm not in. I'm seeing how low the spiral goes!
The treacherous staircase, nautilus shell
interior vortex to personal hell.

There is no mammal inside me.
It's mollusk!
An ectoplasmic massager of the ocean floor.

That is where I am.
And what I deeply am
I record and will report the perils.

Of life outside the Union.
You know? UNION! The merge of Love.
The coupled are up to this.

Or those about to be, with latent love
watchful of,
their niche in another.

In the manual for the machine
of me and people like me
there is a tone to go by.

This ohm I do not own
but it may be S.O.S.
Still I wait.

And I have seen myself
before in the still moment:
when I am the wild animal

and then the tamed animal
and then the lover
and then the lost beloved

and then the vengeful, and then the weary
and in the so-called now, I am throwing out.
Have this! Have what I have found!

Life outside a twisting filament. I am not
lit from within or traveling light. I haven't arrived yet.
That's me, no wait, I'm coming up, over there maybe.

I am mostly broken homes.
Holes on the ground.
In an empty center my true shelf.

That's my name in the whorls.
So it's natural!
Wrong that isn't writing.

Nothing is clear, here.
Hey you! You whoever you are.
Are you in on this?

Tell me. Tell me if you don't mind.
Or have a seat, have whatever you want.
I will watch. You won't even know I'm here.

# THE END OF THE ROAD

Brother I've been so weary as to not even go for the kopeks
in my pocket. Missed the bus twice that way.
A sight in uriny trousers.
(She never made it to meet; what was the point?)

This gets one to the point of "funny looking,"
at which point: look out!
No one wants to eat with you.

Let us forget, for one moment, the siddhas
who eat excrement for enlightenment.
We are not in that league.
We are busy with ignorance.

Furthermore, even if each yammering kook in the public reference
were yogic, I would not want my shirt back after lending it.
Lice are not my friends. I stay up late killing them,
having nothing to discuss.

Elsewhere I have a friend who is insanely beautiful
and largely based in suffering.
Suitors take their skiffs to her shore, but turn away
before disembarking on account of all the fish guts in the water.

I sympathize with all the creatures in this story.

## IN MEMORY OF A MAN

I am away.
Expelled again.

At first, I was not unpleased to leave the so-called stronghold:
The Home. You know how it goes: one must make one's way alone.

I would learn the word self-reliance from you;
I did not learn it personally. I might know it to see it.

You are of little need.
No feast-eater you; no pawn of the Papacy.

We met accidentally. You were hunting
and said I could help. I was retained (a new page).

Thusly busy, I witnessed, distantly, my once-proud people go down.
But I was happy: my head under your hand always ready.

When your lips would be very close to my ear, touching ...
Well that was all I ever wanted; to be drawn closer, necessary.

I wasn't. You were embarrassed by what I must mean.
A fucked-up family. Addle pates touching everyone everywhere.

It's sort of funny considering
the parents' commitment to cover-ups.

Most common urges surfacing
(monkeys and goats).

Everyone knows this.
Everyone knows. You let me go.

So I go with the boys to the ocean.
(The young Crusade!) Well, why not?

They also love someone who is essentially out of bounds.
And they ask about you, oh, sure they do.

And I tell them
you were not much of a lord.

I tell them that you are poor on a horse,
that your form is lumpy like an old woman.

They want to save our soul. You see, they say we are attached.
That we are meant to happen to each other.

They are crazy; I only want to be missed.
For this to occur, one must go off.

The Road.
The nomad home.

I have been seeing people hit the road all my life.
It reminds me that I am meant to wander. Wanting.

Pacing, saying again the things I said, the stupid things
that make me hit my head.

Damn gawky form, damn loose mouth and skin!
That is my sin: holding on.

Remember before?

Are you still into opera?

Do you remember me?

My ability to miss you is my only ocean.

And my soul holds my body too and is a boat too.

I am not bothering anymore to bring it anywhere.

Now I am what's left.

A rat scratching, curious, circling

in the hold with other unknowable beings.

And the men steering this boat will sell us to whoever.
They're killers! We must love them! (The Crusaders say.)

I say your name to put you here.
(They hate us.) Again, I say your name

to see what happens.

God,
we all want another chance.

Everyone around me anyway,
we can't seem to think about anything else.

This I considered to be Love: a chance.

A lasting chance.

What IS that?

What's that smell,

that isn't me is it?

## AN INSTITUTE IS CLOSING

I'm not in with this mystery. Somebody steady me.
Cool ocean breezes don't make me laugh.

I'm in with noisy metal little nils. A million apologies.
I must have made more.

You were sensitive, you needed them.
No you weren't and you didn't. In fact ... oh forget it!

In the middle of the ocean reflected with the moon,
good place to show; probably no one knows you there.

Your leaving, the thrown rope up to sky, climbed up for real goodbye.
I realized my reason insufficient; you must have considered this.

How my specific lean to you smelled like an old paper cup
of funny water and you were not very thirsty.

You came unbidden initially and often. A field
and flickering wicks of foxes from here to there. You.

Holding Hell at bay. Back to ground,
I see you on the moon with your mirror

catching action on the parallax.
Some kind of wise guy.

## THIS WORLD ONCE REMOVED

When you are in a hotel outside your homeland,
remember it is only made for passing through.

I sat upon that phony ancestral bed for years,
voided, holding most close the mysterious
circumstances I claimed fated me.

In comes someone beautiful. I address their shadow,
my gaze and springs loaded. A trip
and I'm off to fight an un-winnable war.

I became a weapon.
My heart an ocean mine
surrounded by my ocean home.

What could I do once I knew this:
that I was wired and hired for love,
terrorized by love—made to play a part

but safely away from any accurate depictions.
All I knew were fictions. Familial reruns.
Codes who go and go.

But the grass tells me it can grow through concrete
because it does. One day
vines will cover every form under the sun

like now but outward. Throughout the groups,
our channels course with "flickering lights"
which rise to merge.

I know this and I don't: my waves appear static
or gross flow of obligation and restraint vs. best intentions

slayed or saved by sleep.

I lie on my side.
I say I'll go anywhere if real love is there.

And then I follow and the promise disappears.
The promise/conjure principle is faulty.
What am I missing?

Stranded on a craft?
Going?
I guess.

The cell door is open.
Sometimes it closes but now it is open

and I do not blame anyone
for going on to their sacred manifestation.
Even if it is without me, it's what I want.

To go to the front of my line,
the glowing trace: the free form after the fall.

# DRY LAND

## SUN ON FACADES

I believe the birds are back.
Swell sparrows of hop and nestle
away one day and so the world went to hell.

These things only register when missing
my friends, I am a hermit.
I do not talk to anyone at all,

except now I guess it must be necessary
to say the sun hitting faces

of buildings against the alluring sky one wishes
to enter. Then breeze to treed lanes
undulant green as ocean.

This sight wants to snuff my utterances
by being the utmost
for my brain today. It says, "Only I say."

One walks watching it
one stumbles; it is like wearing a heavy headdress
and people around aren't into it

so they steer away. Unlike birds
the color of dirt who wish to be nearby
phenomenon.

## LIFE AND TIMES

You Dear,

Come closer and look at me to make me here. Fixed.
Hey, aren't days in this place hazy as Tennessee
or the unseasonal beach or the plain state
elsewhere where is everything.

But what hilts the breast of deer,
what are big-lipped waves saying as they take away,
"sshut-up" or "hussh," "plusss" "sssomething?"

And that southern dog who'd lay around completely.
What guts! Ignoring morning's matter.
Ticked biddings not the sky … phony human time.

The sun we say asserts. Time for deer
bolting back to the woods.
Cease to gnaw the trash heap, we see you.

Humans shoo, scat, etc.
The field responds and the ticks attack—
people lay down with smarting hearts.

What my dog does is base maintenance.
I eye him; climbing.
A point! Is there not a point to approach?

Silence then praise: birds rise and reflect.
A sky scored in silence; they soar and
as they turn down, the dawn has sound.

Pock marks: the target struck: the central flower—

Though what really happened won't go through me
so I can't decently say. I yammer and point.
Get a move on dog. Deer you are late.

I am a timepiece. I must state on and on.
Another state: Now it is night.
An ocean. Nearby, grass on dunes.

Sand hills!
People make love between them.
Each on another.

You are my friend, right?
You know me?
World? Out there?

## WHERE EVERYTHING WAITS

Nobody was left who'd lastly scuffed first earth's crust.
Boiling sea had thin-sheened each cubit of firmament.
Mountains ceased to assert, gave in to ground
arounding whatever hard rock
to then there over and take down.

All shapes breaking hysterical particles and subs who settled
devoting former whir of shape to Silence,
which was enough.

It stayed uniform Silent for some many months
which strengthened to pull outer space noise in to neutralize
but lost its grip.

So this Sound hard-pressed in to sink holes
and look into original force that was still shut in
under black lacquer cabinetry: our future perfect world.

It opened the door of dust,
the space sound picked up pings distantly.
Seeing to sound is what and how Bounceback.

Since the dust so still and small
the waves skinnied high-pitched
to switch on resistance of an average mote.

What would stand to receive?
What was the point of pointing out resisting decay?
What was there to say?

Could anything be activated? Much was strained in "done" state
and so sought exit through the soft Silence under rather than be stabbed
by the point-cornered Silence above.

So sound deranged to be
needle pierce to dust piece
and sunned a word heard first by the bygone ("ouch").

And the Silence startled by the sneaking sound
forgot its own high ground
and grumbled some rebuke.

Underground glad particulates laughed at the gaff and expanded
(something among it a voice) to sweep up what had been.

## PART TWO

One in Dust begun.

One chased out to Perceptivity from mum.

This made an in as such that could close

over after outreach which comes back with something to say.

Stretching comes to the zone where there is shifting

from mixing its own x-space with outside sensed data.

Each already edgy piece in "earshot"

each piece pulled in by dust's desire to harbor more

is similar to dolphin noise.

Riffs that began off flats of static,

f.p. earth (future perfect),

etched by rust-hinged sound.

Not all dust took in.

Those who did not got ultra dense.

If there was a strike to one of this specie

sparks would be three feet at least and atoms unleash.

To them strikes relieve adhesion.

They like hits from nowhere; they won't admit they are hard

in every space.

But sparks in dark if an eye sees them

a mouth to say how beautiful a light of such blue

that lasts and deepens blue.

Shaped like a pin, each spark alights

to hold itself, elsewhere, down.

What it lands on is to remember the spark beautiful.

A spark from Hard Silence made mad.

The more mad makes it harder which gets hit

and flies further because it is harder.

## PART THREE

Minute care is taken so that soft expansive dust gets all over

the dense. Colors change as comes collision.

They want to do all they can now that they can.

Hopefully they don't know about the deep frozen people in orbit.

Those on the figurative shelf until there is a proper place.

More on that after the fire; for now:

the Sound, the Nerve, the Building.

# LOCK DOWN

I have been looking up your words to see who you are
though I know all of you out there are your own special beings
to me you are each in the mansion outside
a different face on each door that is closed.

Despite the press, you all get along together well in life;
relentlessly even in fights.
Both factions show. It is on.
Someone's pulled apart

and then I think I know the way when one element after another
descries its old adhesion and we have here the mess
that won't hold up but that once functioned successfully.
At present, the defeated resemble a puddle of mud.

The beast (me) lopes over; I extend my gristled fingers
like so: going under the dark water to the hard parts.
Well I like them. The, shall we say, shrapnel or pearls
from the (lonesome) former person's own lonesome irritations.

Oh I know you and you me little trophies,
see how I have mine out all the time: the scales,
really these are scales and they go all over
but my clothes cover them, and the teeth—always quitting

at crucial moments. The last time I gnashed them
something, something then I passed out.
Then a voice from behind a door said,
"I can't even hear myself think for all that damn racket."

"Naturally," I said groggily, as their head inside describes
a clear-cut forest plus maybe a resentful memory of a tree falling
and, wait, shouldn't I be hearing something?

The knock, knock, knocking that is the head against it?

I go for my bag. It holds what I contend to be pearls
though they do not pawn or I am more invisible than ever,
a creature below commerce, believe it or not.
Don't they want my business?

"Those aren't pearls they're a bunch of old bones," I was told
by the big man who addresses the man behind me.
"Wrong friend, this is precious. The result of money made.
It's what was first paid." But he won't have it. "Get out!"

he shouts. "No, you get out!" I maintain as he calls for Security.

I am ushered into the day, pushed away, like so.
Born into Hell again is the song I sing at these times.
In Hell we can't reach anyone. We just watch.
They do not see us but we care about them.

They fall apart and we cluck, "Oh I know that feeling, brother," or
"Don't worry, sister, it can't last forever." We are in Hell.
Picture the row upon row of one-person cells.
Almost no one gets a mirror. When we extend a hand—BAM!

"Wherefore art the pain?" sayeth myself unto me.

"Faith, I cannot say, good sir.
Now I only know I am here
and the constant cries, of course."

"Later they will take some of us away."
"But who?" I ask myself.
"And what are they trying to do?"
And myself says,
"It's you they are taking. You, stupid."

"How do you know?" and "What's this business of aloneness?"
and "I'm not stupid,"

and myself says, "Haven't you heard?
Those big embarrassing angels who fought for your carcass
have flown off. Now you are more for rue.

Here is the mirror
but don't put your hand out
as the idiot with the scythe thinks he is independent
and goes for the holders of kopeks of insanity
few and phony though yours be."

## G.

I have been told to talk to you with my head down;
if I did not avert my eyes you would not hear. Weird,
I thought, for the maker of heaven and earth to be so insecure

or to be living here, amidst the stink. Let me start again,
I come in peace in a way being on the side of Life; I am a fan
of your handiwork: flowers, flytraps, burrowing frogs ...

But this is not about that, it is about the demons:
Does everyone have them all the time? Like viri or viruses
which flare when the hope is low?

Or is their manner of attack more bacterial?
Incapable of mere occupation. I guess it digests us.
Laying waste attractions and attachments

with their propaganda campaigns.
A moment while I mourn my blown bridges.
(Sigh.) All right I'm done.

What do the demons see in me? Me, a notoriously poor host;
in my house we sleep on the floor and eat on the floor
but we do not step on the floor; as this is a sore spot.

Maybe they think I want company.
I do not want any company,
not that kind.

After I dreamed the demon was taken out of me,
tornadoes hit Tennessee;
which is where the man who speaks of demons lives.
He said they wanted to get me.

But why? Am I so weak?
Or am I bad? What if I can't love because of them?
What if they are the only thing designed to love me?

You are responsible, G., I am applying again for assistance.
I believe my ground-down teeth and busted guts
are acceptable indicators of my plight
as they are listed in column A

of this application. Which is the fourth I have filled out,
by the way and why is that?
Have I been redistricted to Hell?

Yes? So, that is the point? But you are still at the Helm.
This application is still valid, yes?
I have a right to know what is holding me up!

G., I am tired of living in ignorance with voices and meaningful dreams
after days where everything happened already.
This is the exposé that may put better minds
than mine to these questions.

This is not a joke. Sure I may say it loud; indecorously before
a room of strangers; but that is part of my plan. After all,
they may know something as to this; hitherto unconsidered by me.

Thugs of the spirit world release me!
And You! Maybe the biggest crime boss of all.
Taking care of the people in heaven with their better things
to do, who will sacrifice blood for you and think nothing of it.

Who forced us into particular bodies initially?
You that's who! To play with. To infiltrate.
To pay you back. It's called manipulation, by the way,
those who do it are Creeps.

You see, I am on the wheel beneath your world.
The demons are all about me.
The other people do not believe it; this is not their district.

You made it this way, G., you big bully.
I tell you, you will never, NEVER get away with it!

# FOR THE PEOPLE EXPOSED

Do you realize in this town you are living in
there is someone who is entirely alone
but for a pin/wire arrangement
that connects her to a shock wave?

Never mind that she may have been the author of her delusion,
never mind that she may be lucky not to be an insensate stump,
never mind that she has not yet unplugged the tub of her functioning.

It is fear that prevents her from abandoning her room,
going the soldier road on to the zone: homeless.
The urban nomad plain inside the common street.

She asserted her shadow got sick and lit up
became detached and would not stay behind her
anymore. It seemed to blink at intervals.
She saw the reflection in faces

but the light she could not see.
She only saw them, fleeing, giddy to get into each other,
the people. Off they go, two by two.

She was no longer of anyone.
She was on a stage solo.
Sometimes a face floats by, laughs and goes.

The play, she thinks, is to do with dragons
or foxes. The prop is a feathered crown.
The character is not to be taken seriously, she thinks they think,

and while the clothes on her shoulders faded and her scalp burned
she had no real idea why this was happening.
Alienation is making me crazy, she thought,

but then another coincidence would pull her head up sharply
to eye the sky. Yes. That would be the wire.

It rings her heart
out it stretches for the One to hear.
Tight then dividing. The wire around this thing then things ringing.

Once she wanted a love so big it could hold together every errant piece
of her diced heart. A million pointed pieces
scattered through her travels, her heart

and as each falling heart part may become a star somewhere else
inside her, replacing it, is sand.
That is what nature does—it balances deposits.
The pendulum leaves and retrieves.

What stays is her rickety chest
inside a bloody cup beside a glass of sand
and the rising cry is so far out it is forgetting why it's there
and the pin that holds the wire in, she tugs on it sometimes.

So what?
So what I'm saying is if you know someone like this,
if you know them and you notice these things and you like them,
why don't you be nice to them?
Because they are just about out.

They would like a real friend.
All their other friends are busy with their own crazy stories
and it is cold at the extremity,
blasted, vast and echoing,
this world was not meant to be borne alone.

# NOCTURNE

I am a dog wrestling with a big bloody heart
whose valves flub to the very suck of hell.
Light-footed night and by night welcomed.
Scuffing trees, I am sudden.

Paws upon windowsills, bark rattling citizens inside their turn,
sleeping, sweat-naped, unsuspecting.
If they catch a flash of froth-terrible jaws
in moonlight, they will have taken the present I left.

Taught on night's perch, another moon brights away.
Here's to run where no streets usurp rash brambles.
Here's to find my outer heartland
where small stars hang before the punch is thrown.

## NO SOLDIER STORY

These ghost soldiers live underground with the vast
oversupply of castoff lanterns.
If one were to take broadsword to one of these

orange-bearded mammoth men of rough hew,
he would laugh at the passing metal,
make light of entrails.

For years I have been here without a clear map.
That hopes should dim as days go on above is
natural I suppose, what do I know?

I am dressed like one of them.
The thick walls quake but stay soundproof.
I fear my fists vestigial.

These soldiers' own panic is taking up rugs
finding filigrees of the former world beneath,
e.g., a locket with their mongrel's mush.

They will freeze, then feign noncom; smacking barrels of burgundy
with pistol butts. I react comme squirrel:
fleeing their reach to the chamber out of the impact area.

One loved me until I asked if he worried about what must be
happening without us. Well, his lips did narrow, hand abandoned my knee,
blah, blah big mouth were his departing words.

I will not say with shame that I came from nothing.
Someone paved my first breakthrough at least,

one time calling it love. And I will stand by that
as it applies to my primary makeup.

# HARD EARTH

# THE STUFF OF GOV'T

I was walking with a pal when treachery struck.
What now? The leering many, who hold the reins
to the markets and small food stands
upon which I've come to depend,
have decided I'm odd and so
a threat to the quo and so: poison in the food.

It was late winter when it occurred.
"Could that be a rodent phalange?"
I asked my friend, a known nutter.
He said, "Better take it back."
Yes but no but do you think they're trying to kill me?
And shouldn't I then just play dead
for I'll avoid further assaults on my person?

"Yes, unless there is a network,"
said he from a safe distance.
A Network, yes; it makes sense:
those librarians nearly lethally throwing me
my borrowed books at the old biblioteque.
Que pasa? Is this misbehavior because I am here too often
and they wished I wouldn't be?

Mais oui. How does one deal with treachery?
With the gloomy Gusses and Gussettes
who find a free agent an affront
and therefore care to snuff them.

"I just remembered I'm alive,"
said I two weeks ago, throwing my arms skyward
thereby biffing the appalled Weinberg.
It sounds like nothing but if I had to pinpoint
the commencement of these assassination

attempts, I'd say it was then.

I now think robots run the show.
Inside these guys is a soul tied to a chair.
It gets tortured by electricity:
diode to gonad. I find it sad.
But I didn't set it up.
And of course some souls hardly seem to have a chance,
bu-lah, bu-lah, bu-lah.

Sad, it is too sad, seeing oneself thusly surrounded,
so I sailed off. In this picture I am on an island
thinking of sending up a flare.

It did not occur, the flash that gets the coastguard over.
It's the waiting I hate; and the suspense.
So I rowed on my own to Congress.
"Give me the numbers of the drug companies,"
I demanded. And the Senator said, "They're in the phonebook,"

and I said, "No the real numbers, the meta-numbers, jackass.
I pay your salary!"
And the Senator just said wearily, "Whatever."

He goes inside but doesn't come out.
"Could old Simple have forgotten
the egress?" I says to me.
We shall see and while waiting scheme:
only mad scientist ways can bend the bars
to these mad scientist days.

Hey why not kick the seat of power?
Wherein sits the most tortured soul!
I'm afraid but what more could they do?
They've taken my knishes, even tampered with my soda cans.

"Amigo," I say to the guard, "let me see the big guy."

You can imagine my edges slightly frayed;
my temper very losable.
"No can do." The detector beeps.
"A steel plate," I say.
But I am put in back with a professional woman anyway.
For the deep search.

"Elsa, you've grown ... very beautiful,"
I say. She shushes,
leading me to the tent where we make our discoveries.
She that I am a revolutionary machine, indeed steel-plated;
and I that she is not at all ticklish,
requiring gross charges into the territory.

It's scary. But the perk!
What a buzz to get this one aquiver.
I almost wake her to try it again
though she's complex and might bite me.
Back to the other thing!
First, cloak the camera! Take the tape for later!

Backdoor to the shite house!
I mean White House.
But first is there any gum around here?
Dang, nada. Whatta country.
Are those jackboots in the couloir
or corridor as we say in the stix?
River to Perdition! Everyone outta my way!

As I wade away from old frauhund
to the ghoul rolling bones.
That's him in a picture:
thin-lipped conductor setting the tempo

which nets destruction. Why I oughta …

Indeed, I will kill it with kindness.
And if that ain't effective, a big pretzel
wedged down the gullet.
The Amish call them "love knots."
Why not? It makes sense, they go down poorly
with the conductor considering the carnage.

I'm up in the ducts. Ventilation, I guess.
Listen to the tinny way
it makes sound the things I say.
Plus it's like a catacomb in here.
Skeletons wearing berets,
two clutching each other
wearing floppy leather hats.

"Excuse me comrades,"
I say making my way though I know they're dead.
A sound. Was it movement of motor or decay?
Then a rack of bones pulls away.
"She's here," I hear. "She's come."
What used to be eyes are all turned to me.
"Weird," I say aloud whilst smacking away a withered talon.

They shake their heads and mutter; disappointment.
"Wait," I meant to say,
"what pains you people? How can I help?"
"Oh come on," they say apparently pissed.
They take me to the proper shaft,
after which they tell me it is up to me.
They say testily.

"I hope you have a very good plan."
"I have several," I say, "and they all seem good to me."

"Right," they say as the remains bear me to the head of state.
A simpleton actually, backed by meanies.

I must break the hypnotic hold
of "glamorous saps" with the silver bullet
of sincerity. I must bag his head
and take his shoes away.
"Hey pipe down; we're almost there!"
Loud whisper from over there.
"And may I remind you that we are the army
of Sincerity, not you!"

It made me stop. Where is the fraternal sorority?
Or the vicie versie? I am still going it alone.
I fall off the beam and through the ceiling.
"Throw me a line guys, please?" Nil.
Rat sounds, rat space something, something
their awful race or face would work too.

From the floor I see a cutout of the President
behind which is the President.
He plays a shoot-'em-up video game ... poorly.
His kill shots take the substance from himself—
even the missed ones.
His eyes actually are little red bulbs
lit by an exterior tube.

To pass a hand before them is to have him shoot at you.
I must cut the wires somehow, stop the circuit.
Funny, no thugs are in here—
they will be outside rightly, as they
have no power over what falls from above.

So I'm tugging the plug
and looking around at the man-child's detritus:

silver sporks and steak abound,
a Heimlich sign, La-Z-Boys, and such.
Mostly, though, there were video game versions
of the 50 states, Asia, the former Soviet Union,
things-we-know-are-Evil, and fuel cells.

And McDonald's containers partout.
How does one proceed nonviolently?
How to quietly puke when the wish to expel
settled grub comes up from outrage?
No I can't—and so aim for the takeout container.
A large bucket.

"Texas fried fat skins o' chicken
infused with some mo' hormones
and fed from cow parts and fried again and again,"
says the bucket.
Which I fill with my sick. The President looks up.
Behind his red bulbs fear in orbits.

Is that a tear? Yes I think it is.
Much snot pours forth, poor wretch.
The Government yegs from outside take note and storm in.
(Where are my dead radical friends?)
I'm holding up a handkerchief and wave it around

but it is red.
The bull in them charges forth
and too some German shepherds,
oh Elsa. Gun to head, a quick goodbye.
"I do not want to destroy this guy."
Really my mission was kindness; a show of love.
Pity, a gun goes up where the face was.

# UP AND AWAY!

## ACT I: AGAINST DEATH

Since we are ghosts, since we are barely here
but for pain and song and sad lights from our memories
making it out,

since we are brightest before death …
Wait ghost!
Wait friendly ghost! I'm running after which means I thought of running:

I watched myself do it.
I had regret.
I put it all on you.

You—the mobile ghost.
You—the better ghost.
You with your magic and who am I?

I am an angry friendly ghost. A ghost who wants to lose weight,
one who picks at skin and pulls out hair.
One who doesn't haunt others but who haunts herself.

Ghost among ghosts!
You who are a weary ghost—
who is hungover and scribbling out the fear—
the old buildings that we move through as we dodge machines.

Come here and be faithful to blood,
to the fact that it pours constantly—
the collective blood that pays our way and says almost nothing.

I am haunting these people.
I think they are my friends.
Not well

am I doing this.
I am going to be forgotten.
I do hope that happens.

Maybe then I can change,
maybe I can say:
You go here, do this do that:

first A, then B, then C
and I will be reliable
as for endeavor.

But always it is:
C! B?
Fuck you A. I never needed A.

A is destroying my mind—
A is the devil and the devil wants to fuck and crawl out of me again;
to make me responsible for the end of it all.

A—the thing to do—
avoid the devil,
do the laundry.

Avoid the devil's cameras.
Hi! I say. I smile.
Behind the loudness, my evasion, the hangover, I am planning,

planning to get better.
I am figuring somewhere else.
I have been working on it.

I've been imagining the woods—not the city.
The woods and within the clearing
two castles.

They will dig me out from a whole.
I was sleeping inside a tree.
You see I killed myself before for love. I could not be found.

Others needed me and I did not care.
I needed me but I did not know it as I was essentially leaking
everything and the love and the pain it mixed

sand to glass inside—it broke and my glass with wine
broken—this is how I drank it.
This is what shocked my voice

this is the further tear along the front.
The front filling up with blood—ballooning with it.
It fears the air a bit.

It needs to keep moving.
Wary blood, how can I blame you.
I am dead.

I did kill myself. I must forgive everyone in pain.
I must give them everything to correct my mistake.
It isn't easy. Sorry.

Well, the furies,
you know—the furies who can cure them?
They have many arms all weaponed, all holding edges and points to tear.

You can't hug them from behind.
They roll with spikes out.
Who's in there? What blood is in there? How can it be freed?

I am part of you furies.
I am a radiant of you too.

Let me take you in and care, a fire is fixed for you.

My sister in her car.
We will die now, I thought.
We're together—it fits.

I guess I'm ready,
if this is love
it isn't trusting.

Love you are allowed to be you.
You with frightened blood and plagued
by cameras from beyond and dancing sort of.

You with no magic
that has become a new magic
of ticks and clicks. Hit it with a stick.

Metal, it is now,
a moment! I have stopped,
aware of my complete apparent lack of comfort.

Numbers. Points in the dark.
Heaven. Old time.
Shame. Shame the stupid soiled person, the actor.

You out there, there is a way.
A way to break out!
You mate with flames

You forgot—

You forget

You must have been

You must be:

A. Devil

B. Angel

C. Motion

D. Dog

E. Electric

F. Made by Men

C. Computer, broken circuits cutting other circuits

inside and around

outside holding you in.

Inside screaming

Your Friends are keeping you here,

They need someone too, Love.

LOVE TERRIBLE LOVE

LOVE TERRIBLE LOVE

STAY WITH ME

## THERE WAS A BIRD OUT THERE

Yes, there was a bird out there, a bird I could be.
It looked like dirt: a sparrow, a niche taker. I loved it.

It hopped more than it flew and when it flew,
it flew briefly. Over and up—

away from Danger
or to the heart of it.

She looked like her companions so I named her.
What won't be still inside me is what calls to you, little birdie.

The breath took the words to the world and swirled about the greater air.
But my beloved was hurt.

That is me slightly
significantly.

I went into the world to bring her home.
I went into the hole in the world that connects my heart.

I opened as much as the bird might need
but she was hurt

and not up to flying straight or seeing a home
through that blue light I summoned,

so I prayed the name to shimmer the trees my dear bird seeks.
I waited with my light while dust entered me I became of dust—a husk.

My child a stalk of corn that dried without drought so it grew no more.
And the grain on the stalk grew mold because it rained.

That shocked me. It lowered all lights.
And mold grew over the portal I was holding.

I better get out before the catastrophe.
To enter through me now is to catch decay.

That was my dim hymn,
my faith betrayed by me.

My light, where was it? It has gone before you.
So my will closed the whole thing down.

The tower of entrance—the beckoning of one bird
is not for this mouldering tower. I am a single straw—this moment.

Machines distantly cutting down my friends and others.
Those who just like me used to glow as favored sons.

These keening machines: their frenzy is to fool you.
They are harried for no good reason.

Meanwhile the grain, germs, and seeds,
below a coating of mold, sleep-stained, awaiting

fire prime. How can one get inside
when one is all but gone from retraction?

I am here in the dark.

I have a turning heart; I cannot fly far.
I live distantly it is dark.

My love this is what remains for you: a bough.
The branch to be received by. Something true.

# EACH DAY DIFFERENT ENOUGH TO BE SOMETHING THE SUN CAN STAND

These crows we see manifest ill crowd mentality.
If their going off in pairs is as mate, does it as love redeem?
I'm afraid no. This tree too unhappy full of messy noise;
i.e., crows.

When a dead man dries his soul gets to go
with wind. Hawks come in
against crows in a wheeling tournament for soul.

If the black birds get it; they celebrate in a tree
to scare it, living, under them. No moonlight gets past them;
much less a helpful sparrow.

If hawk, talons out to prize—
if hawk wins, soul goes higher privately.
Dust souls have nothing to say about it.

They only want enough weight to be worth the effort.

I see today getting dark. Villagers walk home quickly
according to the state of the sky. They urge each other
in as well I'd want myself, in general. In, that is.

This world is large insofar as it has
a big grasp to take the unattached away
which attracts certain animals.

Maybe you think this emphasis on hypothetical phenomena
with questionable qualities just as well not there.
But you said "Big World" yourself
and not without the look of an imminent ice bath.

I have told those turned cold to go.
I want to stay myself but more informed.
I want the animals to like me.

## I'M AMAZING, I'M A FIREMAN

And there was a field of battle
not two blocks from my place
in which they tussle
and gain and lose rank.

I remember my mother suggesting
the path at the edge which avoided the worst.
We are not shy people, she would say,
we're quiet. We go this way.

Upon my soul! That will never do! I'm wound up!
Look! I can, I can, I can!
Fury?
Flurries of pride more like, the mother would say.

I run to the fight. How like a cold ocean its blows.
I lash out many times. Where am I again?
A thud to the head, a thud to the head.
Success here I come!

Slowly the will goes away. I roll down a hill and like it.
I open my mouth for filth.
I pray I never stop. I'm only going.
A slow nut spinning in a parking lot.

I come to at the Clinic—
a blood test, a boxed lunch, it's baloney.
It's my mommy, I say,
waiting, waiting, waiting, I fade.

Buzz in the head. Pulse outside.
The beating of the field itself.
It holds hearts. The powerful pump

blood into its dirt inadvertently astounding it.

Mainly I feel fright in the air, metal.
The shimmering leaves are vectors for falling.
They are living messages. In times of war they are rarely read.
Etched in green shoots, the messages miss me.

They appear to be speeding through that phase
of searching out the sun.
What convinced us—
what convinced me

—although I may not be convinced—
what convinced me of the cage
was waking up in it and not knowing anyone.
After the intake I was told to go home and wait.

They will see me tomorrow. "Do you know who I am!?"
I say inside, "Do you realize who you are handling!?"
I go to my home, my substation. Everything must be rearranged!
It must be touched, its dirt examined. Only I decide who stays!

I'm a flame!

I'm a card, a king!

A burning king card with a heart!

With many hearts.

# THERE IS ALWAYS A WAR

*for Scott R. Johnston*

Good Lord: A Tree burning and budding
arising from a corpse at its base—
a suicide with a soft spot for shade.

Miracle mind. It wants a place to go.
The girl, on fire and fear, replaced herself.
To the Branches go blood vessels.

A reaching hand—
light through leaves.
Stereotypical peace, PLEASE.

Hey what's that? What hums?
A chainsaw to slay her decomposing place.
Reenter the fear—

"Now I can't get away at all,"
the dead girl said to no one apparent.
"Oh God, oh God, oh God, save me."

By the context she is meant to stay
and so she is staying.
This tree, air, and dirt situation will hold her

until she is ready again to enter her chariot.
Slowly, she will receive messages.
As an old form breaks, her pieces scream out for Love (see me!)

and it is bounced back to her:
Her persistent Frequency!
Her Own Beauty, Her Own Love is picked up.

Human High Voltage!
Alone one is a spinning top not spinning,
e.g.: a bug stuck; though inside it is avid.

With others we shoot colors and hum.
Landscape of Receiving and Exchange.
Open but it needs.

Record, reorder. To know, to have value.

To be with it. To be with You.
To be You. Acting it out;
or throwing it against these walls

amid mounting shadows. You discrete parcels, You people
waiting to be opened; to share what is inside.
Oh You! I am going overboard for you!

Because I do not know you I am mingling too much.
It's heated and particles are fleeing.
The fusion drone: There is no ALONE!

The melting down boundaries, ADIOS!
It's instantly everything!
It's instantly over!

Leaving a panged being.
To be among it all.
To fly surprised like a spark

is to become a dog who waits by a door
for the best One,
skeptical of the return.

How can I contain myself?

Well I am not containing myself.
My reactor is leaking, there is a crack in my core.

To be alive is to itch all over, I find.

My friends, my psycho foes, no longer know me.
They reinforce their outer limits with many skins.
Sweatered, jacketed, and capped with metal:

wrapped thusly THEY WILL NOT BE DISSOLVED
like a lozenge—refined disc to mouth.
They would spit that concept out!

The alien mouth may take them and say something crazy.
The alien mouth may misunderstand.
They might be smeared.

And they are only themselves:
everything apart from the alien mouth. No don't go there, they say;
dark matter caught here.

We wait with them; becoming them sometimes.
Fear audible and visible but among it, LOVE
cutting shapes.

Who are you here?
Where's the gag generally present at this distance?
The unfanged laughter?

A-hum-in-a-hum-in-a-SUMMONING.

Hello! Life! Hello! Glowing squid-like mind!
Where do you go
when you go?

And how can you amid the suffering!
The tearing and shredding.
The insanity.

Okay, let's breathe together, things are changing right now.

May I give you some Hope? Some Love?
HERE!
Here, a place to put your fear; go ahead.

It's a velvety basement with a dragon motif.
Clattering trash can lids:
sound of fear putting its feet up.

I see this place, it isn't bad.
I'm not worried about anyone stuck here.
Hell, I'm stuck here: a Leaf at the end of a Branch.

There I go falling into the miracle night with You and Lucky.

## FOR YOU I WILL MAKE MYSELF USEFUL

My word, you rats are lonely,
you who run through my mind.
You are stinking, so I am stinking!

Song of discomfort! My thing!
You who may be there; what could I give you?
Words well done? Idiocy prevents me.

How's this: Ish Klein loves you X (genuine signature and date)
and can lend a limited amount of money to you, in your time of need.
If that is what you want.
Or I will make physical contact.

How far will we go? You tell me.
Wait! I should arrange these things, these words, or whatever.
Polish the brass.
Words:

The sun is like an omen.
The moon, a variable drip.
My heart is like a tire fire.
You who read this are like a beautiful drug.

And I LOVE drugs!
It's the year of the dog; the drugged dog.
That's my year!
My hand is now a puppet calling out to you.

What else do I have for you?
I can tell you where I found money once.
At this place I also found a pack of cigarettes.
Outside the Central Library. Left facing South. Apparently enchanted.

Okay, enjoy this flat mechanism which is maybe in your hand.
Save it until you find a use for it.
Love, Love, Love,
Ish Klein

# THE PHASES

You were exposed to a great light briefly before development;
not a word convinces otherwise as you see
the various lights around others.

It is not for classification.
Necessary, it lets you in on this:
the purpose to be close (light) remember.

Your first house was shy on light, has kept you little
as some plants are little as the functions done for them:
cup of dirt, some water, pull off the dead parts.

This type tends to stay small
as for need, seeking just enough light. So what?
All light is puny compared to the first (remember).

Who found you in the dirt,
discounting aloud your brain's lack of lift,
she could say such things because she did.

(Anyone can and why not?)
What's more this weirdo wanted you to love her.
It was easy. Getting fixed for human use.

Then she was off to make fun with other frumps.
A Tesla-type, a light fixture.

But you went back to scuttling over sidewalks;
a box over your head and only one eye hole.
Regress, the sweaty head. Hey!

Are you not made to be free near trees primordial
such as one from Tasmania?

Or are you more moth-like, guided by the moon
and often off course?

A light is on you genius; a light you grew bent searching for
and all around you the wildlife dare you to stand up for it.

## ONE GOES AWAY

Whatshisname tried too much of everything and rang a bell
of dissolution that reached the people
before his own physical entrance.

Schlubbish he'd become as a decadence;
noisily wiping his nose with his hand that once handled snakes.

This man who'd jumped his destroyer in '44
amid chum and pieces of pilots with the "Lemme at 'em!" intent.

Inside his mind he was biting the side
of a great white shark face.

He made bloody the sight of himself there in the Pacific.

Sharks knew what his type tasted like,
they could take him, but why bother?

Fresh as burnt rubber the flesh;
certain pills of which tasted of condemned liver,

the sharks would later puke. And if smaller fish ate that,
that they might later eat—well it would be an even worse bellyache.

So they let him be, gliding off to take pilot meat,
charred but not bad and less likely to repeat.

Such was this galoot, kinked sinister with whisky and foul mouthed,
but he had a quality that moved me—

his eye had been all about watching God's
every move and in this endeavor he had been quick to laugh.

Who knew he would hold, once older, so much pus around his heart
or that his scars would curse the fields of his skin?

His good eye, long gone lazy, shut.
I would visit until one day he said I was a pervert who knew no beauty

beyond "Freak Show." I disagreed
and he showed me the door.

"What's that for? I'm a friend."
But that was the end.

I took to walking around towns.
More natural disaster than national holiday.

Then I sped up and was unbecoming on bicycle;
there were no mansions in the distance, no signs saying where

I'd find the bigger picture the lines in my right hand prefigure.

Soon I met the goon who said if I remain true
to only two dimensions the end of my line
would be an edge and I would fall off.

He said I was a fool who must learn to conceive
and I'd better believe heartily in every dimension
if I want to get anywhere in one piece.

I regretted having met this man because his words hurt my journey.
I couldn't move. Why do I listen to loons?

I asked myself this for days and made a song about it
which I will sing at the end of the world
during the high wind and fire phase.

I was mad and my bike broke
so I had to walk

and a dog ran after me
so I had to run

and I fell in a ditch
so I had to play dead

and then that dog howled and would not stop.

He blamed himself. I had to do something.
"Look, I'm alive! Sorry for faking," I said.

He was startled but he stayed, a peacemaker.
Finally we slept after our strenuous day.

In a dream we are running,
I think in a stream,

and he changes the race to pounce
between rock life and water life

connecting both with a paw placed in the middle
of their range

his bone below to recognize the rock
his blood comes up to the water.

Being with everything is natural for him.

So we are different

but I am there

and I am running among water

and I am breaking apart

on the screen of this dream

which is actually not bad

I hope I never come back.

## THE GARDEN

And the humans saw themselves in a puddle.
It was lighting in the sky.

They were checking out the scene:
considering the human span.

They watched the layers take over:
containment by clothes. Swaddling first, the birth place,

buffered. Holding close. A baby makes its way off its mother
by choice, in a perfect world.

This world isn't perfect but it's enough.
Anyway, no colony was way more wild than another.

Each had the fear and the wrong idea often.
Each shot people into the sky.

Each goes to hell in a certain way and tells about it—
maybe it's helpful, maybe it's made up, maybe they are mean.

The face on the mask determines behavior even after
the mask is put down sometimes. Wait a minute! This was a play.

Costumes hold power, though. People put on tight bright wrappers
to inflame hunger (their own) for someone else's eye.

Some would want to eat a bowl of their own substance.
Some would serve.

What does the human actually own? A flowing, a flickering.
Its form and voice occur by cuts and sorting. Nothing personal.

It isn't yours. So high so low. So hello!
So low and hi! Phasing this way and that.

The argument ensnares and entwines and a child comes out of a channel.
It was a kind of fight; it can be frightening, choppy, what-next type dread.

The kid will speak up in its form.
It gets what it says it deserves. Maybe a new mask is made: an honor,

a dance to get out from under.
To find why you, step this way.

By your view and appetite;
hunger is always hanging around.

In the face of the shimmering pool someone sees young animals take place
inside human eyes. This is the puddle watcher again; the guy in line one.

S/he says, "The ones I'm from are young. We don't know much."

And all around the tree leaves lift a little to let more light down.
This human thought it won something and said, "I love you."

It was darker again and in the puddle—

WAIT! Did I mention the garden is in the battle field? Inside a medical tent?
Because it is. Did I say the human had a wreath and a golden rope?

In the battle as a lasso it couldn't really kill anyone
and it couldn't let them go.

It pulled a certain person close. They read each other's face.

They ate from different plates
but at the end of the day they each took up the same amount of space.

"Get out of my face!"
"Get out of MY face!" they said for ages.

And they whipped each other with the frayed ends of their golden ropes
and they each tried to recover their wreath from the other one's throat.

What a wreck this field of battle was.
But the volcano liked it because it could relate

and the worms who sucked the blood from the mud,
they were happy too. They had food.

And the comical rats who'd like to live in human skin—
with a corpse they come in through an eye (a little bird taught them).

At the appropriate moment they say, "Lookee, lookee I am brilliant,
I have a human brain that I ate. And now I am on top!"

Ha ha ha go those simpatico. They roll down the aisle.
Theatre of the oppressed or of those with a bum rap: very close,

overlapped even. The rat comedy, the human tragedy.
Those inside the medical tent can't care about either.

Did I mention they take turns looking at the puddle?
(The fighters from lines 33-48 or so.)

Now that they are both down, they check it out.
When one is done the other uses the rope

to pull their opponent's head up.
The wreath around each neck digs in.

For them it's less painful than the little words:

please, enemy, please.

There's a speech in the rat comedy about this.
Bittersweet, I'd say if I weren't out of my depth.

But I'll go on. I'm in luck: nobody holds me.
I can see the tent people.

Sometimes they let the end of their rope fall over into the puddle.
Somewhere else the gold rope appears, it's frayed and delicious looking—

the tassel as from corn. The spirits climb to eat it.
Reaching the zone—they are overcome with commotion:

two tangled warriors wanting more.
There's nothing to eat for them, not much to see.

What a bore, they think, and watch the rats for a while.
I wave "hi."

How did I get in on this? I tried and tried to shine.
I told the spirit, "I love everyone, potentially."

"And in the now?" the Spirit asked.
I evaded, not knowing the right answer.

My halo was going down, the wreath I mean,
the choker, I tensed the rope

but the spirit pulled that collar off my throat and asked,
"Why are you holding in knots this line that lets you fly?"

The spirit showed me the grove. Its trees hold orange suns.
I throw my rope to be of radiance on its behalf—my try at love.

Well I'll be! Lightening I was,
illuminating an area. It was too new to me; I looked away.

I went back to
the home I used to have.

A man was there trying to finish his food, he was dropping off.
This basement, his bucket, his home.

I used to live there.
It has a rat annex.

That drove me crazy,
I remember.

A man, a red rose. That is, an inflammation of hope. The rose.
Each try soaks red through when his loneliness doesn't go.

When it turns to hurt and he stays
for the next turn, that is the famous rose

or lotus that's the light blue generator
in the middle, the miracle. I see it!

Bouncing on my rope, where did his go? His rope?
The spirit held me as I lowered.

"He threw his rope to you long ago,"
I was told.

And so, I became the gold rope.
I let myself go until I touched the blue jewel at the center

and still, I kept going through.
I reached and reached that he might feel it.

My light to his flame, we can take it,
we don't only hold it, we don't blister.

In the blue-based flame its rise says red and brightens and then
cools to a green branch which holds an orange—the taste gold.

The memory: the mouth resonates, smiles, says yellow,
the thought of a smile is violet it's free,

the light with everyone free—a white light
we meet to be made new,

a lamb for a while, a man too,
sometimes a girl is you tasting grapes,

making spirits, laughing,
moving among it.

Each person who holds their own frayed hand
out to the frayed end is holy, electrifying the whole.

In my book they get to go to the place that needs them most,
the place that would save them.

The gold rope, the wick pierces a flower's heart
to be blue this way of flame is to be new always.

In my book everyone can always be new
if they want to.

Friends this place has a garden; your heart has a flower.
It is in the teeth of mystery,

it's exploding as we speak.

## ACKNOWLEDGMENTS

For previously publishing versions of some of these poems, grateful acknowledgment is made to the editors of *Gare du Nord*, *The Canary*, *The Hat*, *Spork*, and *XConnect*, as well as Dottie Lasky and Linh Dinh, who posted poems on their blogs.

Thank you Josh Edwards, Robyn Schiff, Nick Twemlow, and Lynn Xu for your great talent in making this a real book.

# ABOUT THE AUTHOR

Ish Klein lives in Philadelphia. She attended Columbia University and the Iowa Writers' Workshop. She is also a filmmaker.